A Book of Reptiles and Amphibians

A Book of
Reptiles and Amphibians

BY CHARLES PAUL MAY

ILLUSTRATIONS BY JOHN CROSBY

ST. MARTIN'S PRESS   NEW YORK
MACMILLAN OF CANADA   TORONTO

J
598.1
M

To R. D. and Helen Timberlake and their family
and to Kenneth Ricker

Contents

Each chapter begins with a drawing of the fully-grown adult of the species. The drawing at the end shows, in most cases, the eggs or the young.

A Book of Reptiles and Amphibians

Introduction

Millions and millions of years ago a fishlike creature crawled from a warm jungle lake. It came into a world so different from ours that we can only imagine what it was like. There were many plants, but no birds and no mammals.

In the water behind this creature swam many fish. From the water they absorbed oxygen through their gills. Gills contain many blood vessels near their surface. As water passes over the blood vessels, the oxygen from the water goes into the blood. Waste gases leave the blood and dissolve in the water which is passed out through the gills. Taking in oxygen and getting rid of waste gases are the main steps in respiration.

Out of the water most fish cannot breathe. But this first fishlike creature, to leave the water successfully, had developed lungs. Now it could breathe air and stay out of the water.

After millions of years passed, the descendants of that animal breathed air more easily and could travel away from water. They were no longer fish. They were amphibians. This word comes from two Greek words meaning "both" and "life". Amphibians are animals that live first in water; when they are adults, most live on land.

Although they breathe air, amphibians must return to water to lay their eggs. The young hatch in the water and have gills. As they become bigger, they go through a metamorphosis (met-a-MORF-o-sis), or change. They lose their gills and use their lungs. Then, like their parents, they live on land.

None of the early amphibians exist today. Most died out altogether. Others changed further. After more millions of years and by many gradual changes, they became frogs, toads, and salamanders.

Certain amphibians developed into a different kind of animal. This animal laid eggs with a shell, which kept the egg from drying out. This type of egg would not hatch if laid in water. It had to be laid on land. This animal we call a reptile.

"Reptile" comes from a Latin word meaning something that creeps. Most reptiles in the world today have short legs or none at all.

Although amphibians came first, reptiles in time

"ruled" the land. Some of them became huge. And there were great numbers of them. As they increased in size and number, they became the main animals of the world. For this reason, we call their major period on earth the Age of Reptiles.

The largest were the dinosaurs. This name means "terrible lizard". We still have lizards, but no dinosaurs. None of the "terrible lizards" of the Age of Reptiles are alive now.

The turtle, one type of reptile from the Age of Reptiles, is still living today. Bigger turtles but much like the ones we know today crawled over the land during the time of the dinosaurs.

Reptiles have scaly skin while the skins of amphibians are smooth. Reptiles feel dry to the touch. Amphibians often feel moist. The scales at the ends of reptiles' toes become claws. Amphibians lack claws but may have sticky pads on their toes which they use when climbing.

Turtles differ from other reptiles. They have shells as well as scales. The top shell is called the carapace and covers the turtle's back. The underneath shell, known as the plastron, may cover the belly completely or it may not.

Reptiles and amphibians are known as cold-blooded animals. Birds and mammals are able to keep their bodies at a fairly stable temperature. But the temperature of the bodies of reptiles and amphibians changes with that of their surroundings. This is partly because they have no insulating coat of fur or feathers. When snakes or turtles become cold they bask in the sun, or if they become too hot they move into the shade or burrow underground. Only in this way can a reptile or amphibian keep its body temperature at an even level.

When winter comes, reptiles and amphibians hibernate. They go into the ground below the frost line or into the mud to keep from freezing. There they sleep until spring.

Reptiles and amphibians have eyes similar to those of mammals. Reptiles, particularly turtles and snakes, have better sight than amphibians. Snakes have lidless eyes. Because they lack lids to close over their eyes, snakes always seem to be staring. Even when they sleep, the snakes' eyes are open.

Reptiles and amphibians have nostrils. It is doubtful, however, that many of them have a good sense of smell. Snakes and some lizards use their tongues to help them test their surroundings for odours. This explains why they flick their tongues in and out of their mouths. Tiny particles in the air or on the ground stick to their tongues. These are placed against sense organs in the roof of the mouth. The snakes are then able to "taste" the smells around them.

Reptiles and amphibians do not have visible outside ears. Yet these animals have eardrums. These are just beneath the surface of the skin and may be noticeable as round areas below and behind the eyes.

All these creatures suffer at the hands of man. By draining marshy lands and causing forest fires, man destroys the natural homes of reptiles and amphibians. Sprays, meant to kill insects, also kill these animals, and so do careless motorists on the roads. Most reptiles and all amphibians are harmless, and they help man because they catch large numbers of insects. As you learn about these animals, keep in mind that they are worth protecting. Let us hope there will always be reptiles and amphibians on earth.

CHARLES PAUL MAY

Leatherback Turtle

Many tales have been told of monsters seen in the oceans. Many such reports are false, but some large animals do live in the sea. A few of these are reptiles.

One of these, the leatherback turtle, is the largest turtle in the world. Huge ones reach a length of over eight feet and may weigh between 1,500 and 2,000 pounds. More commonly they grow six to eight feet in length and weigh 750 to 1,000 pounds.

These giant turtles spend most of their lives in warm water near the equator. But in spring and summer when the warm ocean currents flow along the coasts of the United States and Canada, leatherback turtles may swim north. They are regularly seen as far north as Nova Scotia and British Columbia.

If you see a mammoth turtle at sea, look for a ridged, leathery back. Among salt-water turtles only the leatherback turtle has these ridges.

Where most other turtles have bony shells, the leatherback has a top cover of skin. This leathery coat gives the animal its name. The colour for an adult ranges from dark brown to greenish or greyish black. A young leatherback turtle has light yellowish spots on its neck and lower jaw.

The leatherback is more at home in the sea than any other turtle and prefers the deep water far from shore. The male leatherback never comes to land but the female leaves the water on a moonlit night to lay her eggs.

The leatherback has limbs meant for swimming. They are paddle-shaped flippers without claws. The front pair has a span of eight to twelve feet. The leatherback cannot walk on these flippers but uses them to drag itself across a beach.

Somewhere in the tropics, the female leatherback finds a nesting site. Above the high-water mark on a beach, she digs a pit two to three feet deep with her hind flippers. In this bowl she lays sixty to eighty white, round, soft-shelled eggs. She covers the nest with care, and then churns the sand over a wide area until you cannot tell where the nest lies.

The young hatch in six weeks to two months and are only two to three inches long. Although some baby turtles cannot dive for a few days, little leatherbacks can submerge soon after they hatch. In the sea, they catch jellyfish and shellfish.

Leatherbacks are ancient reptiles. Their ancestors first appeared over two hundred million years ago, long before the dinosaurs. While dinosaurs have long been extinct, these turtles have adapted well to their life at sea and have survived.

Painted Turtle

If you want to watch painted turtles, stay quite still. When you move, you make the ground shake. Humans can't feel the slight vibrations of the earth, but turtles can.

Painted turtles live in southern Canada from British Columbia to Nova Scotia. In the United States they can be found all across the north and in most of the central states.

They live in still or slow-moving waters. Ponds, swamps, small lakes, and sluggish streams attract them. You can find them in ditches where water stands throughout the summer. Few turtles live in so many places. Since they dive at the slightest hint of danger, many painted turtles may live near you without your knowing it.

Find a log or some rocks partly submerged in a pond or marsh. On a hot, sunny day sit motionless several feet away and watch. A dozen or more turtles four to seven inches long may crawl onto the log or rocks to sun themselves.

Their heads and necks are streaked with green and pale yellow. Around the edge of each turtle's smooth carapace will be red markings, while the shell itself will be green or brown to black.

If you could see the plastron, or bottom shell, it would be tan to bright yellow. This bottom shell reaches almost to the edge of the top shell. The painted turtle can pull its head, legs, and tail out of sight between the two shells, but it cannot close the bottom shell against the top one as a few turtles can.

In the south, painted turtles may remain active all year. Farther north, cool days after mid-October force them to hibernate for the winter. They sink to the bottom of their watery homes and burrow into the mud or under leaf mould. They may also use old muskrat houses or holes and cavities in banks. This winter sleep ends after the middle of March or in April.

Painted turtles catch water insects, dragonflies, flies, and beetles. Now and then they eat small frogs and fish. Dead animals also serve as food, as do water plants. These reptiles eat under water. Turtles do not have teeth. The edges of their mouths are bony. They tear their food into small pieces with their beaks and feet.

A male painted turtle courts a female by swimming backward in front of her. He waves his front feet before her or lightly taps her face several times with his sharp claws.

Late in the afternoon, some time between May and July, the female leaves the water to lay her eggs. On rising ground in an open space she slowly and carefully digs a hole with her hind feet. While laying five to twelve white eggs, she seems unaware of anything around her. Then the female covers the nest and smooths out the dirt. Unless raccoons, skunks, or squirrels locate the eggs and eat them, the young turtles hatch in about six weeks.

In the north the babies sometimes stay in the ground until the following spring. Once they appear, they attract rats, weasels, crows, hawks, and owls. If they do get to the water they have a good chance of living for ten years or more.

Painted turtles are among the most widely distributed kinds of turtles in North America. In most places, they are the commonest as well. But they are shy and timid and therefore hard to find easily.

Snapping Turtle

Don't step on that rock! It bites. More than one man has stepped on what he thought was a rock and discovered it was a turtle. The snapping turtle in particular has a dark brown, rocky-looking carapace.

The top shell of the snapper consists of rough ridged plates, on which little water plants often grow. This shell may be a foot to two feet long. The small cross-shaped bottom shell only partly protects the neck, legs, and tail. It is yellowish in colour and has no markings.

Down its long tail the snapper has a series of upright plates. The greenish-black legs, neck, and head are rough. The head of the snapping turtle is large, with an upper beak that hooks down over the lower one.

That big head can be dangerous. When attacking, the snapper thrusts out its head too fast for the eye to see. When the wide-spreading jaws snap shut, they can shatter a bone or snap off a finger.

On land, this turtle viciously protects itself. A grown snapping turtle can fight off most animals except a human. In the water, the snapper doesn't attack. Instead, it retreats from danger.

Snappers live in almost any body of water – ponds, lakes, and rivers. The hardy snapper can stand a surprising amount of cold, but in winter it hibernates. Under water, beneath a covering of mud or vegetable debris, it sleeps through the coldest months.

In the United States look for the snapping turtle east of the Rocky Mountains. In Canada it may be found in southern Saskatchewan, Manitoba, Ontario, Quebec, New Brunswick, and Nova Scotia.

A walking snapper seen from the side looks like a prehistoric creature with armour on its back. It holds its body well off the ground. While its walk is awkward, it is not slow. It often walks on the pond or river bottom instead of swimming.

To catch food, the snapper swims up under a water bird, grabs it by the leg, and drags it under. Frogs, snails, crayfish, small fish, and small mammals also serve as food, and these reptiles eat dead animals. Water plants add variety to their diet.

On a May or June morning, the female sets out to nest. Like other turtles, she digs a hole with her hind feet. The twenty to eighty eggs are tough and springy.

Skunks and raccoons eat the eggs when they can find the nest.

Baby snappers hatch in about three months, though in the north they may spend the winter in the egg and hatch the following spring. Most young turtles have the same enemies — especially crows, hawks, foxes, and skunks. Only when hibernating between October and March are small snappers safe. If they escape their foes, snapping turtles may live as long as twenty-five years.

Spotted Turtle

Unlike the snapping turtle, the spotted turtle rarely bites. When it is touched, the spotted turtle pulls legs, head, and tail into its shell and remains motionless until left alone. In the wild, it is more timid than the painted turtle. Any slight vibration or movement sends it to the bottom of its pond, swamp, stream, or ditch, where it hides in the mud.

The spotted turtle resembles the painted turtle but is even smaller. The carapace is three to four and a half inches long. It is black in colour but each section of the shell has at least one round yellow or orange spot on it. The turtle appears to be wearing a polka-dot carapace. As the turtle grows older, its dark-brown head, legs, and tail also show yellow or orange spots. The plastron is yellowish, blotched with black.

Like the painted turtle, the spotted turtle basks in the sun on logs and rocks. It often shares basking places with painted turtles, but it lives in a much smaller area of North America. Watch for it in the states along the Atlantic coast, especially south of Maine and north of South Carolina. Pennsylvania, New Hampshire, Vermont, Ohio, Michigan, and Indiana also have the spotted turtle. In Canada, you can find it in south-western Ontario.

Where moist woods or pastures occur, spotted turtles sometimes live for days away from bodies of water. Under such conditions, they probably eat little or not at all. Usually they eat when in the water. They catch tadpoles and small frogs as well as water insects. Dead fish also serve as food.

These reptiles are among the first to come out of hibernation in the spring and the last to go to sleep in autumn. They sometimes appear early in March. More often, mid-March to mid-April finds them coming up from the mud of still or slow-moving waters. They remain active until October or even November.

The female lays her eggs late on a June afternoon. If bothered while digging the nest or laying, she pulls into her shell. Some turtles seem completely unaware of danger at such a time, but not the spotted. Once her two to four eggs are laid, she covers all traces of the nesting site.

When the young hatch, two and a half to three months later, their top shells are nearly round. Only one yellow spot shows on each shield of the carapace.

20

The small shields around the edge lack spots at this time.

With many turtles, it is difficult to know a male from a female. But you can recognize a male spotted turtle by his dark-brown eyes. The female has orange eyes and in general the markings on her head are brighter than those of the male. The male grows a tail an inch and a half or more in length, while the female's tail remains less than an inch long.

Wood Turtle

Can laws save a turtle's life? They have saved such animals as the bison and the whooping crane from extinction, so let us hope they can save the spotted turtle and the wood turtle.

Both of these reptiles are becoming rare, especially in the northern part of their range. While many other turtles stay in or near water, the wood turtle lives much of its life on land, where man is its major enemy.

Even men who do not intend to kill wild animals may cause their deaths. Men who clear or drain land to expand city suburbs or build summer cottages unknowingly bring about the death of various reptiles.

When turtles are caught for pets, they usually have no further chance to produce young. Here legislation should be able to protect them. In some areas, such as New York State, laws forbid people to catch wood turtles for any purpose.

23

Wood turtles are found from Virginia north through New England and into New Brunswick, Nova Scotia, and sometimes southern Quebec. They also inhabit moist, wooded areas or damp pastures of certain parts of southern Ontario, as well as Michigan, Wisconsin, Pennsylvania, and West Virginia.

This is one of the easiest turtles to recognize. The large shields of its carapace stand up like carved pyramids of brown bone or wood. They are encircled by rings. The yellow plastron, blotched with black at the edges, is well developed. It reaches almost to the edge of the carapace on all sides. When the turtle pulls in its bright orange-red legs, neck, and tail, it has good protection.

On a newly hatched wood turtle, the carapace may be wider than it is long. But as the reptile matures, the top shell reaches a length of seven to nine inches with a width of only four inches.

Start watching for wood turtles late in March or in April. You will find them in berry patches, mushroom beds, and orchards as well as swamps and ponds. In addition to eating fruits, berries, and tender leaves, they catch snails, worms, and insects. By late October you aren't likely to find wood turtles, for many of them burrow under rotting vegetation or mud before the end of September.

24

Sometimes the young hatch just before it is time to hibernate. The female lays five to twelve white eggs in mid-afternoon between late May and late June. They don't hatch for three or four months.

Turtles usually make only faint sounds, if they make any. These may just be hisses as air escapes from their lungs when they pull quickly into their shells. But the male wood turtle whistles. The female also whistles, but the noise she makes is faint while the male can be heard for many yards.

Alligator Lizard

Lizards look more like the ancient dinosaurs than either snakes or alligators do. Bones of lizards have been found in rocks formed during the Age of Reptiles. But lizards, of course, are a great deal smaller than dinosaurs.

Take, for instance, the alligator lizard. The head and body together may reach a length of five inches, while the tail adds another five to eight inches. Like most lizards, its legs are short. It stands no more than an inch and a half high.

Men have named it after the alligator because it is supposed to look like a tiny one. Its snout is a trifle longer and more pointed than the snouts of many other lizards. But the scales that cover its body are part of the reason for its name. Like the scales of an alligator, they have keels, or ridges.

An alligator lizard shows dull colours. The scales are mainly brownish grey to olive-brown. Here and

27

there on the animal's back, black scales give a speckled appearance.

These lizards are found in both Canada and the United States. In Canada, you will need to go to southern British Columbia to look for them. In the United States you can find them along the western coast as far south as northern California and westward to Montana. They are also found in the Big Bend region of Texas.

As it moves slowly through fields and woods, the alligator lizard looks for grasshoppers, millipedes, beetles, and spiders. You might mistake it for a small snake until you see its legs spread wide at its sides. Its body wriggles as a snake's body usually does, and its slightly forked tongue flashes in and out of its mouth.

The alligator lizard must watch out for snakes, large birds, and some mammals. Like most lizards, it doesn't see its enemies clearly. It sees movement. If something moving toward it is too big to eat, the lizard runs away.

An alligator lizard is sometimes caught by its tail. But the tail breaks off. In fact, the alligator lizard loses its tail so easily, it may shed this organ without being touched. The lost tail wriggles for a while. If the enemy is attracted by the tail, the lizard has time to reach safety under rocks or thick brush. Since it is slower than many other lizards, the alligator lizard is often saved by its tail. A new tail grows to replace the one that is shed. But each new one is shorter than the one before it.

Lizards that live in the north often differ from those farther south. A lizard in the tropics can lay eggs in a warm place and leave them alone. The sun's heat will hatch them. Suitable warm places in the north may be less easy to find. But lizards that carry their eggs in their bodies can move about to find warm spots.

The female alligator lizard carries her eggs inside her body. The eggs hatch inside the mother. Then the young are born. They have no further need of the mother and all of them go their separate ways.

Five-lined Skink

As you walk through the woods, listen for movement among the dead leaves and plants. When you hear a rustling stop and watch for the animal making the noise. It may be a nearly black lizard with a bright-blue tail. Perhaps it will be a greenish-grey lizard. Or it might be a dull-brown or olive-coloured lizard with an orange head. Any one of these can be a five-lined skink.

When this lizard hatches, in July or August, its body is dark and shiny. Its beautiful blue tail looks as if it should belong to another animal. Five yellowish stripes run down the lizard's back, from the head to halfway along the tail.

During its first two years, this lizard changes colours. The blue of the tail and the darkness of the body fade until the five-lined skink becomes greenish grey. The stripes turn whitish or silvery. The small, smooth scales of its skin still shine.

In five or six years, the five-lined skink grows old. You may not be able to see the five lines any more, and the scales no longer shine when they catch the sun. The female becomes a dull olive-grey and so does the male except for his head. The head of an old male is orange.

The five-lined skink inhabits moist, wooded areas. In the United States it lives in all states east of the Mississippi River except Maine, New Hampshire, and Vermont. It can also be found west of the Mississippi River to Texas. In Canada, look for it in southern Ontario.

Five-lined skinks of the south grow to about ten inches in length. Those in Canada may reach only six inches from their short, rounded snouts to the pointed tips of their tails. The tail accounts for about half the length of the lizard.

Warm days in April or May bring this lizard out of hibernation. It searches for worms, flies, ants, beetles, caterpillars, spiders, and new-born mice. Like other small lizards, it must flee from snakes and birds. Skunks, bears, opossums, raccoons, rats, hogs, dogs, and cats also catch it. For short distances it can run fast. If the five-lined skink gets caught by the tail, the tail breaks off. A shorter one grows to replace it.

Some time in June the female lays six to eighteen eggs under a log or among fallen leaves. Instead of leaving her eggs, as most lizards do, she guards them.

She turns them often with her snout and defends them against mice and other small creatures. After she has been out in the hot sun, she may curl around them so they are warmed by her body.

The babies are about an inch long when they hatch. They can look after themselves immediately. Chilly fall days send them into the ground to sleep. In Ontario they must burrow deeper into the ground than they do in Georgia to escape the cold of winter.

Short-horned Lizard

Most lizards are long and slender, but the short-horned lizard is broad and short. Instead of a long tail, it has a tail that adds only an inch or so to its three-inch body. Because it looks like a toad, it is sometimes called a horned toad, but it is definitely a lizard.

Like other lizards, the short-horned runs. Its body is flat, and when frightened it may flatten its body even more. As it lies motionless in sand or on a rock, an enemy may pass by without seeing it.

Their grey, brown, and yellow colours help short-horned lizards to look like the sandy or rocky areas in which they live. In Canada, they can be found in the dry sections of southern Saskatchewan and Alberta, and British Columbia. In the United States, you will see them in many of the western states, especially Montana, Wyoming, North and South Dakota, and north-eastern Colorado.

Few animals feed on these lizards. Some of the scales on their heads develop into spikes, or horns. These seldom hurt an animal's tough outer skin, but they scratch the soft lining of the mouth. Even so, a hungry snake will swallow a short-horned lizard.

Short-horned lizards are not dangerous, yet they act fierce to frighten enemies away. They stretch up on the claws of their toes and puff themselves up with air to appear bigger. Sometimes they hiss like snakes. The bravest ones attack and bite, but an enemy hardly feels their little cone-shaped teeth.

The short-horned lizard has a "secret weapon". It can squirt blood from its eyes for a distance of about seven feet. When an enemy comes toward it, the lizard forces blood into the region of its eyes. As the pressure builds up, a thin wall of skin splits, and the blood shoots out in a small stream. It may drive the startled enemy away.

The short-horned lizard can go many days without food. If the temperature drops below seventy degrees, it won't eat. But when the temperature is high, it looks for ants. It also eats flies, spiders, and moths. At times it searches for food, moving slowly. Or it lies on rocks or half buried in the sand waiting for insects to come near. As they approach, it shoots out its long, sticky tongue and captures them. To drink, it runs its tongue over damp leaves.

The short-horned lizards of Canada and the northern states carry their eggs in their bodies. The female gives birth to a dozen young at one time. Farther south, the female digs a nest in which to lay twenty or more white eggs. After covering the half-inch-long eggs with sand, she leaves them. The sun keeps them warm until they hatch.

A short-horned lizard that lives in the north usually buries itself at night to stay warm. It pushes its nose into the ground, then wriggles and squirms its way beneath the surface. When cool fall days arrive, it no longer comes out to eat. You won't see it again until late the following spring.

Bullsnake

"Hiss-s-s-s-s-s-s-s." Was that a steam pipe exploding? No, it's only a bullsnake warning you to stay away.

Few reptiles make so much noise. The bullsnake can be heard a long distance. It breathes forcefully against a thin sheet of elastic tissue in the back of its mouth. The tissue vibrates, just as the reed in a clarinet or saxophone vibrates when you blow across it.

"Hiss-s-s-s-s." If this doesn't drive an intruder away, the bullsnake gives the appearance of being fierce. It coils its body and shakes its tail, as a rattlesnake does. The tail, of course, makes no sound. The bullsnake also lifts its head, weaves it back and forth, and suddenly thrusts it forward. Unless the snake is really frightened, it doesn't bite.

When these actions fail to scare an enemy, the bullsnake may bite. Since it has no poison, the bite is harmless. Yet any person who is bitten by any animal, even a pet dog or cat, should put disinfectant on the punctures. The teeth of animals carry bacteria, and some of these "germs" might cause infection.

If small animals are near, the bullsnake makes no sound. It glides under a barn floor or through the grass of a pasture searching for mice, rats, ground squirrels, small rabbits, and gophers. Finding one of these, or a small bird, the bullsnake catches the creature in its mouth. Quickly it loops its body around the victim. It is a constrictor – a snake that coils around its prey and squeezes tighter and tighter. When the animal stops struggling, the bullsnake swallows it whole.

Because it kills rodents, such as gophers, rats, and mice, the bullsnake is one of the best friends a farmer has. No wise farmer kills this reptile.

Bullsnakes are most numerous on the Great Plains. Look for them from southern Alberta and western Saskatchewan south to Texas. Some live east of the Mississippi in Illinois and Indiana.

Large bullsnakes reach lengths of over seven feet and they are among the biggest North American snakes. Usually bullsnakes are five or six feet long. The head is a muddy yellow spotted with black or dark brown and has a dark line from the eye to the jaw. The back shows large black to rusty-brown blotches streaked across with yellow. The sides show more yellow, and the belly is mostly yellowish. As the tail tapers off to a point, the black and yellow areas separate into rings. The tip of the tail is black.

As with turtles and lizards, you won't find bull-snakes in cold weather. They hibernate in small caves or animal burrows. With the tough scales on its snout, this snake can force its way into a gopher mound until it breaks into the tunnel beneath. After catching the gopher, it may spend the winter in the deepest part of the tunnel.

When bullsnakes come out of hibernation in the spring, they seek mates. In July, the female makes a shallow burrow in a sandy spot. Here she lays a dozen to two dozen eggs that are a bit smaller than an average hen egg.

About two months later, baby bullsnakes from a foot to eighteen inches long break out of the eggs. Like other reptiles they look after themselves immediately. They are full grown in four or five years.

Common Garter Snake

The common garter snake lives in a great variety of places. Even in city parks and vacant lots if there is grass and moisture, you can sometimes find these attractive reptiles. In the country, they live in meadows, woods, marshes, roadsides – usually near water.

Garter snakes can be found all over North America except in the extreme northern parts of Canada and the island province of Newfoundland. They are the best known and most common of all our snakes.

You will recognize a common garter snake by three stripes down its back, one down the centre of the back and one down each side. With most of the snakes, the stripes are yellowish, the central one being especially bright. But they may be light brown, yellow-green, or even blue. Between these light areas is a dark ground colour. It also varies, sometimes being black but now and then appearing to be dark brown, dark green, or olive in colour. The belly is always lighter than the back and may be greenish to yellow.

The female bears twenty or more young in July or August. Some female garter snakes have produced nearly eighty young in one litter, but this is rare.

The new-born snake looks wormlike, with a slender body and a length of about five inches. Birds find it good to eat. Other snakes eat the babies and even full-grown garter snakes must watch out for other snakes larger than themselves. The bad-smelling liquid they give off when attacked doesn't save them.

During their first summer, the young garter snakes grow rapidly on a diet of worms. Before they crawl three or four feet down into a crack or hole in the earth in late October or early November, the young ones have grown half a foot. During the winter sleep, they grow hardly at all. In spring, they are among the first snakes out of hibernation and once again they grow rapidly.

Now they eat more than worms. Frogs, toads, snails, tadpoles, and small fish form part of their diet. Like other snakes, garter snakes don't necessarily eat every day. They probably eat best when temperatures reach the eighties, and the food a snake swallows one day may keep it satisfied for several days. During their second summer, garter snakes may grow another foot and they will be fully grown when they are a foot and a half to three feet long.

All snakes shed their skins at least once and often several times a year. Even after they are adults, they continue to shed, but not as often as when they are maturing. The old skin peels at the lips and the snake wriggles out. Sometimes you can find these discarded skins. They are brittle and almost colourless.

When she is two years old, the female garter snake can produce young of her own. From now on she adds little to her length each year and may live fifteen to eighteen years.

Western Hognose Snake

If reptiles were given awards for "acting", the hog-nose snake would probably be the winner. When an enemy approaches, it gives a "performance" that often frightens the intruder away.

The hognose snake spreads the ribs at the back of the head. This gives it the hooded appearance of a dangerous cobra. The hognose puffs out the rest of its body with air to appear as large as possible.

While spreading its head and neck, the hognose snake hisses. If the enemy comes closer, the snake jabs its head forward. But it rarely bites.

If this fails to drive off an intruder, the hognose snake goes through other actions. It flops about as if dying. Its tongue trails out of the side of its mouth. It rolls on its back and lies completely still. You might think it was dead, but if you turn it over it quickly rolls onto its back again. There it lies until danger seems to be past. If a quick look around shows that the enemy has gone, the hognose rolls onto its belly and glides away.

Because of its bluffing movements, it goes by several nicknames, such as puff adder and spreading adder. Many people fear it as a poisonous snake and kill it for this reason. Actually, it is harmless.

There exists a mistaken belief that any snake with a triangular-shaped head is poisonous. If this were so, the hognose would be one to watch out for. But this is not so. Another belief is that thick-bodied snakes are dangerous, but this isn't true either. There is no need to fear the thick-bodied hognose snake. If you live where there are dangerous snakes, find out just what they look like and avoid them.

The western hognose snake is becoming scarce over most of its range. It can be found in southern Manitoba, Saskatchewan, and Alberta as well as in the central United States Great Plains region and south to central Mexico. There is also an eastern hognose snake that can be found in most of the eastern states and in southern Ontario. It is similar to the western species.

Sandy areas serve as home for hognose snakes. They also live in fields and orchards. The turned-up scales at the end of the nose, which give them their name, are used when the snakes burrow. They search underground as well as on the surface for toads, their main food. They also eat frogs and tadpoles and a few insects.

The female lays eighteen to two dozen eggs in late July. The leathery shells of these eggs are elastic and stretch as the baby snakes near the hatching stage. On breaking from the shells, the plain grey young are six to eight inches long. They eat more insects than grown hognose snakes do.

By the time they are fully grown, hognose snakes are a foot and a half to almost three feet long. The western hognose snake is yellow-brown with dark-brown blotches on the sides and back. The belly of the snake shows heavy black markings.

Playing dead

Massasauga Rattlesnake

Why are there so many false stories about rattle-snakes? Perhaps it is because most people don't care to look at them closely. Since they are dangerous, this is wise. Only a herpetologist, a scientist who studies reptiles, should try to study rattlers. The rest of us should learn about them from this scientist.

Contrary to some stories, you cannot tell a rattle-snake's age by the number of sections in its rattle. The rattle consists of thin scales at the end of the snake's tail. Each time the reptile sheds its skin, a new set of scales can be seen. The segments fit together loosely and make a buzzing sound when the snake shakes its tail.

Each section of the rattle represents one shedding of the snake's skin. In its youth it crawls out of its old skin two to four times a year. As it matures, it grows less and sheds the skin less often. The older segments of the rattle become brittle and may break off.

Rattlers eat mice, rats, rabbits, birds, frogs, lizards, and salamanders. They have good sight, but rattle-snakes also locate prey with unusual sense organs. On either side of the face between the nose and the eye is

51

a pit that is sensitive to heat. The warmth from another animal's body lets the rattler know the animal is near by. Snakes with this sense organ are called pit vipers.

One of the rattlers found in both Canada and the United States is the massasauga. The name comes from an Indian word meaning "big mouth". Rattlesnakes can open their mouths so wide that the upper and lower jaws make a line almost straight up and down.

When a rattler opens its mouth to bite, two long, curved fangs swing down from the roof of the upper jaw. These fangs are hollow, and the snake's venom – or poison – comes down through them when the snake strikes. After the venom kills a small animal, the snake swallows its prey whole.

The poison also helps to defend the rattlesnake against its enemies. When disturbed, the massasauga usually crawls away, but it will strike if threatened.

The massasauga's colours are dark. It is grey to brownish, covered with black or dark-brown blotches. The belly is black with whitish or yellowish markings in no set pattern. A few of these rattlers may be solid black.

Another name for the massasauga is swamp rattler, as it often lives in swampy areas and moist grasslands.

It can also be found in dry woodlands. As wet areas near lakes are drained for summer cottages and camps, it may move to drier land.

This thick snake grows two to three feet long. The head has a somewhat oval shape, and nine large scales cover the top of it.

There are eastern and western and desert massasaugas, but only the eastern species can be found in Canada. It lives around the lower Great Lakes region. From southern Ontario, its range extends down through western New York and Pennsylvania and through Michigan, Ohio, Indiana, Illinois, Wisconsin, Iowa, and Missouri. The western and desert forms of the massasauga range as far south as Mexico.

In late August or September, a female over three years of age gives birth to about a dozen young. If they can avoid hogs, hawks, owls, men, automobiles, and disease, they probably live twelve to fifteen years.

Eastern Milk Snake

If a farmer sees a snake around the barn on a day when he doesn't get as much milk as he thinks he should, he wrongly blames the reptile. For this reason some snakes go by the name of milk snakes.

A milk snake seems to have less fear of humans than some other reptiles. It enters barns in search of mice and rats. For the same reason, it crawls under porches or houses and has gained another name – house snake.

All down the smooth, shiny back and sides of the eastern milk snake are blotches of red or coppery brown. Every reddish-brown area has a thin border of black. White to yellowish or tan spaces separate the blotches. Just behind the head may be a yellowish Y-shaped or V-shaped mark, but this can be missing. The snake's belly shows spots of black and white in no regular pattern.

Look for this attractive reptile in the northern and central United States from the Atlantic Ocean to the Mississippi River. It is also found in southern Ontario and southern Quebec.

Many types of country provide the milk snake with a place to live. Open fields, rocky areas, woodlands, river valleys, and even mountain slopes can be home for this reptile. It spends much of its life in hiding, under barn floors, loose boards, rocks, or logs.

It is not a mid-day reptile. It comes out to hunt only after the heat of the day has passed. It may continue to look for food until well after dark. Like the rattlesnake, it has fairly good night vision.

Catching a mouse, small rat, lizard, or bird, it quickly loops itself around the animal. Like the bullsnake, it constricts, or squeezes, its prey.

A milk snake eats other snakes smaller than itself. It has some immunity to the venom of poisonous snakes, so it can feed on them. As a result, people make the mistake of thinking it searches especially for rattlers. It probably eats the young ones when they cross its path, but mostly it lives on mice. Because of this, it is one of the best friends a farmer has.

The female milk snake lays six to fifteen white, oval eggs early in July. She deposits them in a hollow in the ground, or under a rotting log. When the eggs hatch early in September, the young are seven to eight inches long and are blotched with red.

The babies eat insects as well as other small animals. And they may be eaten by other snakes and by birds. Milk snakes act like rattlesnakes when they are approached. They vibrate their tails, which, of course, make no sound, and they hiss. They are not bluffing. They strike quickly, and sometimes they bite without warning. Although they are harmless, the bite of an adult milk snake can be painful to a human.

When fully grown, an eastern milk snake will be two to three and a half feet long. During the summer months it eats many harmful rodents, thus making it one of our most beneficial serpents.

Red-bellied Snake

Few people see the harmless red-bellied snake, yet it is often considered dangerous. It doesn't look like any of the venomous snakes. However, it has a bright-red or yellowish-orange belly. Many people wrongly think that any snake with a lot of red on its body is poisonous.

This snake's back may be olive-brown, brownish yellow, or such a dark brown as to seem black. Behind the head are three yellowish spots. This area is known as the nape.

If you find one of these shy foot-long snakes in your neighbourhood, you can be sure it will be there all its life. You may never see it again, but it probably stays within a few yards of where you saw it.

Perhaps this area will be wooded, but with the trees growing some distance apart. Or the reptile may live in rocky grasslands. Every state east of the Mississippi River has some red-bellied snakes, but they may be found in one part of a state and not in another. The largest groups of them can be found in the highlands and mountainous parts of the north-eastern United States. They are also found across most of southern Canada eastward from Saskatchewan.

During most of the day, red-bellied snakes hide under rocks and logs. We seldom see them because of their secretive habits and their small size. When they come out late in the afternoon or just before dark, they may be attacked by skunks, hawks, owls, or larger snakes. If left alone, they search for slugs, snails, beetles, and worms.

In July or August, a female red-bellied snake that is two years old or older gives birth to a few young. She may have only one or two a year, which is most unusual among snakes. Or she may bear fifteen to twenty young. The babies are three to four inches long.

Red-bellied snakes hibernate by mid-October. They crawl down into cracks in the earth, into the tunnels of small animals, or into caves. Because they are slender, they can force their way through the runways of an anthill. Once four feet or so below the surface, they settle down for the winter. Dozens of red-bellied snakes may share the same sleeping-quarters, which may also be occupied by garter snakes.

Ringneck Snake

Sometimes a nest of many eggs means a female produces a large family. At other times it means more than one female has used a nest. Among the ringneck snakes, several females may lay their eggs in the same spot. They usually deposit them in July.

If you find two or three dozen small eggs in a rotting log or under decaying vegetation, they may have been laid by three or more female ringneck snakes. Each female lays a few to a dozen eggs. As the material around them decays, it gives off heat, which helps to incubate the eggs.

The eggs absorb moisture from their surroundings and swell. After eight weeks or so, the snakes inside split the shells with a small tooth that grows from the centre of their upper jaws. Most baby snakes have a shell tooth, but many of them break from the egg by wriggling and don't use the tooth at all. Within a few hours, or a day or two, they shed the tooth.

On hatching, the little ringneck snakes are three to five inches long. They will grow until they are a foot to eighteen inches.

When young, the ringnecks are quite dark except for their reddish or yellowish bellies. In a couple of years, when they are mature, they will be somewhat lighter. Their backs will be dark grey to blue-black while their bellies will be yellow.

The most noticeable mark is the one that gives the snake its name. The ringneck has a yellow stripe around its nape. It looks as if it's wearing a golden collar. All its scales are smooth, without ridges. They would shine in the sunlight if the snake came out by day.

Like the red-bellied snake, the ringneck remains in hiding much of the time. You would have trouble finding it for this reason. At dusk or after dark it crawls from under the rock or log where it has spent the day.

As it moves slowly through the moist woods where it lives, it seeks worms, beetles, and small frogs, lizards, snakes, and salamanders. Like all small reptiles, it is hunted by bigger ones – especially other snakes – and it is caught by birds of prey.

When approached, the ringneck uses its colour to try to frighten an enemy away. It suddenly twists its

64

tail into the air so the yellow underside will show. If the enemy doesn't take alarm and retreat, the ringneck may wave its tail about like a danger flag. Since these snakes are secretive and not easy to observe, it is not known how helpful this display of the belly colour is in protecting the reptile in the wild.

In addition to its show of colour, the ringneck gives off an unpleasant odour. This may give it some protection from foxes, raccoons, and skunks, but probably not so much from birds and larger snakes.

The ringneck snake can be found in southern Ontario and Quebec and much of New Brunswick and Nova Scotia. In the United States, watch for it all through the eastern and many of the central states.

Water Snake

Water snakes live from the eastern edge of the Great Plains to the Atlantic coast. They are more numerous in the eastern part of their range than in the western section. Most plentiful is the northern water snake. In Canada, it can be found in the south-western corner of Quebec and in southern Ontario.

From southern Maine to southern North Carolina and west to Nebraska and Kansas you can find the northern water snake. Along the edges of ponds, lakes, streams, and rivers and in swamps and bogs this snake makes its home.

People kill the harmless water snakes thinking they are poisonous. No doubt they are sometimes mistaken for the dangerous water moccasin. But the water moccasin, or cottonmouth, is a southern snake. It overlaps the range of the northern water snake only in south-eastern Virginia, eastern North Carolina, western Tennessee and Kentucky, southern Illinois and Missouri, south-eastern Kansas, and north-eastern Oklahoma. In the south, don't get near any thick-bodied, dark-coloured snake that is in or near water.

The northern water snake's stout body grows two to four feet long. It has a short, narrow tail. The upper half of the snake's back usually has large dark-brown blotches separated by tannish areas. The tail region is banded with wide brown bands and narrow tan ones.

The belly of the northern water snake will be yellowish to whitish. It is spotted with dark-red or black half-circles or uneven blotches. As a water snake grows old, all its colours become darker and duller. The brown and the tan areas may blend until the snake appears to be plain dark brown to black.

Since the water snake spends its life in or near water, can you guess what it eats? Frogs and fish make up a large part of its diet and it also feeds on tadpoles, toads, salamanders, and crayfish.

Although it swims well on the surface of the water or just below, the water snake usually cannot catch fully grown, healthy game fish. They are too swift for it. If any of these fish are swimming slowly and cannot escape the snake, they are probably sick. The water snake does the fisherman and the rest of the game fish a good turn by catching these ill specimens before they cause diseases to spread. The snake may also prey on catfish, which are not game fish but are slower-swimming scavengers.

Water snakes are active by day or by night.

On warm days they often sun themselves on ha[ ]
submerged logs or on the branches of bushes or lo[ ].
hanging trees that extend over the water. At any
unexpected vibration, they drop from their perches
with a plop. They swim underwater to a reedy or
brushy spot where they can surface without being
seen easily. They can remain below the surface of the
water for many minutes at a time.

In August or September, a female northern water
snake gives birth to twenty-five, fifty, and sometimes,
even seventy or eighty young. Their seven- to nine-
inch-long bodies are brightly coloured. Because they
can be seen easily and are small, they must watch out
for enemies, especially larger snakes.

If cornered, northern water snakes defend themselves fiercely. They flatten their bodies and strike
angrily. When possible, they flee swiftly to the nearest
body of water.

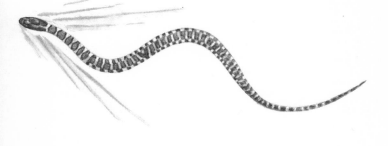

Bullfrog

"Jug-o'-rum!" The call booms through the evening air for half a mile. The male bullfrog makes the sound by forcing air from a vocal sac under his lower jaw. The female doesn't call, but she squeaks if caught. Both sexes may give a "surprised bark" when they become aware of danger and leap into the water.

The enemy might be a hawk, owl, skunk, raccoon, opossum, snake, or human. In the water, the bullfrog may be caught by water snakes or fish. If possible, the frog swims to the bottom and hides among plants or debris. With nostrils closed, it absorbs oxygen from the water through its skin and can stay submerged for long periods of time.

The hind legs of the bullfrog are good to eat. To keep this amphibian from being completely destroyed, in some areas, laws against catching it have been passed.

The bullfrog ranges throughout the eastern part of the United States except for northern Maine and southern Florida. West of the Mississippi, it ranges from Nebraska to southern Texas. This amphibian also lives in southern Nova Scotia, New Brunswick, Quebec, and Ontario.

Man has taken the bullfrog into other places as well. You may see it in southern British Columbia and in the United States west of the Rockies.

The bullfrog is North America's largest frog. Its body looks wide and flat. A full-grown male may reach a length of seven inches, though four to six inches is more common. The females are smaller.

The dull green colour of the back and legs will help you to recognize this frog. The throat and belly are greyish white. The yellowish, large bulging eyes become especially noticeable at night when a light strikes them.

The front feet of the bullfrog lack webs, but the hind feet are webbed nearly the whole length of the toes. The fourth toe on each hind foot sticks out beyond the others, which is the case with most frogs and toads.

You can find bullfrogs in ponds, quiet sections of streams, and swampy areas. While many frogs seem to prefer small bodies of water, bullfrogs sometimes live in good-sized lakes. They eat almost anything that moves and is not too large. This includes insects, small fish, crayfish, salamanders, and even mice.

Among the last frogs to come out of hibernation in the spring are the bullfrogs. They wake up between March and mid-May. In two weeks to a month after they appear, the females lay their eggs. One female may spread a sheet of 25,000 eggs on the surface of a still pond, though 10,000 to 18,000 are more common. They are held together by a jellylike substance.

In the heat of the sun, the eggs quickly grow. Where days are long and hot in the south, the tadpoles wriggle out in four or five days. But in the cooler parts of North America they take up to three weeks to hatch.

Fish and aquatic insects feast on both the eggs and the tiny larvae, or tadpoles. And the growing larvae are caught by water snakes, large aquatic insects, fish, and other frogs.

The tadpoles hibernate without having turned into frogs. The following summer, the larvae continue to grow. In the south, the change from tadpole to frog, or metamorphosis, probably takes place at this time. But in the north the tadpoles still do not change. After another winter of sleep, they become frogs. No other North American frog takes so long to lose its gills and tail while growing its lungs and legs.

Leopard Frog

Like a leopard, the leopard frog has spots, which give it its name. These spots are brown, while the general colour of the frog's smooth skin is greenish to brown. The spots on the back are rounded and have thin, pale borders. On its legs, the leopard frog has brown blotches. From just behind each eye, a yellowish ridge of skin runs down the back. The frog's belly is plain white.

There are many nicknames for the leopard frog. A logical one is meadow frog, because this amphibian often spends its time seeking insects, worms, and spiders in moist fields. Frequently, it lies in wait until something to eat comes along. Its sticky tongue darts out and catches the victim.

Although the leopard frog has small teeth in its upper jaw, it cannot chew food. The teeth help it hold the animals it catches until it can swallow them whole.

In a meadow, a leopard frog may be caught by a snake or a raccoon. The glands in its skin secrete a liquid that some animals find unpleasant to the taste. Most amphibians have this protection, but it does not always save them from their enemies.

When not in grassy or weedy pastures, the leopard frog will be in or beside water. It finds places where grass grows to the water's edge. If approached, it springs far out into the water. It may be the champion jumper among North American frogs, because it is able to cover three feet, or thirteen times its own length, in one leap. The big bullfrog jumps only about two feet at its best.

The northern leopard frog lives as far north as the south-western Northwest Territories. Look for it in all of the Canadian provinces except northern and central British Columbia and Newfoundland.

In the United States, it lives in all the northern and central states but only in the eastern parts of Washington and Oregon. In the east it can be found as far south as northern Georgia and Alabama, and in the west it ranges down through New Mexico and Arizona into Mexico. California has the northern leopard frog only along parts of its eastern edge.

This frog comes out of hibernation early in April. The males soon start making grunting sounds to attract the females. A leopard frog has two vocal sacs, one on each side of the throat just over the front legs.

The females lay loose masses of eggs in still waters in April. The young hatch in May or June and change from tadpoles to frogs in July or August. In October, northern leopard frogs sink to the bottom of ponds and streams and burrow into the mud. Dozens of them sometimes hibernate together. They will not suffocate in their muddy homes for frogs can absorb oxygen through their skins.

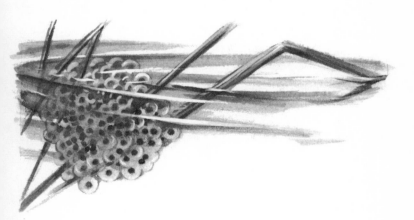

Wood Frog

When ice still clings to the edges of pools, you would not expect to find reptiles and amphibians awake. Yet the sturdy wood frog may be heard – "quack, quack, quack" – calling for a mate. His ducklike voice carries only a short distance, so you must be quite near to hear him.

In general, the wood frog is an amphibian of the north. Although a few can be found as far south as Georgia, you will discover they are more numerous north of that state. They live in the central and northern states between the Mississippi River and the Atlantic Ocean. West of the Mississippi you can see them in Minnesota and north-eastern North Dakota.

All provinces in Canada have wood frogs except for the island of Newfoundland. This frog reaches into the Northwest Territories, the Yukon Territory, and Alaska and even lives above the Arctic Circle. No other amphibian and no reptile on our continent can survive so far north.

The males call the females as early as January in the southern part of their range and as late as April in the north. By April or early May, each female has laid two to three thousand eggs. In round masses the size of tennis balls or baseballs, they are usually attached to plant stems near the edge of shallow pools.

As soon as the eggs are laid and fertilized, the adult frogs leave the water. They spend the rest of the summer catching insects in the moist ground litter under trees. Those that live where there are no trees hunt among the bushy shrubs of their territory.

Inside the jelly, eggs develop rapidly into tadpoles. The temperature can fall as low as thirty-seven degrees without killing them. The wood frog tadpoles wriggle out of the eggs in three to five days. Although they are now free to swim about, they are not highly active for another two or three days. They feed on the larvae of water insects, algae, and microscopic plants and animals until they grow into frogs in July and leave their pools. By the time they are fully grown, they will be an inch and a half to three inches long.

Adult wood frogs are tannish to pinkish brown. There is always a dark-brown narrow line from the snout to the eye, which widens behind the eye into a large triangular patch. To some people this marking looks like a robber's mask. A pale-brown ridge extends down each side of the back. The sides are lighter coloured than the back, while the belly is lighter still.

Some wood frogs seem to fade as summer passes. In the fall they are a lighter colour than when they first appear in the spring. But the dark blotch, or "mask", across the eyes remains clear and will help you recognize the wood frog.

Chorus Frog

At times it sounds as if all the frogs in a neighbourhood have come together to call. The males of all species of frogs have distinctive calls that you can learn to recognize just as individual bird calls can be learned. Frogs have two calls – a mating call and a cry of distress. The mating call is used to attract the female.

Among the frogs that become specially noisy are the chorus frogs. Because many call at the same time, they sound like a chorus. But there may be several inches or several yards between the callers. Some will be hidden in grass, while others may be squatting in shallow puddles.

There are many kinds of chorus frogs. The one that lives farthest north is the boreal chorus frog. "Boreal" means "northern". These frogs can be found as far north as Great Bear Lake in Canada's Northwest Territories.

Chorus frogs also make their home in eastern British Columbia and eastward to Ontario. In the United States, look for them in all of the states from New York south to the Gulf of Mexico and west to Arizona.

"Pr-r-reep, pr-reeeeep!" call the males. Some aren't more than three-quarters of an inch long, and the largest reach just over an inch. The females may be slightly larger but they won't be more than an inch and three-eighths in length.

When a female joins a male, they enter shallow water – a pond, shallow lake, marsh, or roadside ditch. As the female attaches her eggs to the stems and leaves of the water plants, the male fertilizes them.

The calling occurs when the first warm rains of spring arrive. This will be in March or April in the south and later as you go north.

Unlike bullfrog tadpoles, the larvae of chorus frogs develop rapidly. As with other frogs and toads, the hind legs appear first, one growing out on either side of the tail. The front legs grow at the same time, but they remain hidden inside the body at first. They push through the skin shortly before the tadpole's tail disappears. Metamorphosis takes place during the chorus frog's first summer.

Chorus frogs have slender bodies and pointed snouts. Compared with many similar amphibians, their legs are short. As a result, they hop instead of taking long, frog-like leaps. Only a little webbing grows between the toes.

In general these amphibians are dark greenish to brown. Greyish to olive-brown stripes or dots run down their backs and along their sides.

Chorus frogs are in the same family as tree frogs, but most of them never climb anything higher than weeds or small bushes in their search for insects. The small disks at the tips of the toes of the chorus frogs secrete a sticky liquid that holds them to the weeds. In the tree frogs these disks are well developed.

Spring Peeper

Hear the "jingling and the tinkling" of the spring peeper? "Eee-EEP, eee-EEEEP." The shrill whistling peep ends on a rising note and is quickly repeated several times. If you are half a mile to a mile away from a group of chorusing males, the calls may sound like the ringing of small bells.

Around and in a small woodland pool, a group of males may gather nearly side by side on a warm night. After they come out of hibernation with the first warm rains of spring, they call to attract female spring peepers. In the southern part of their range, these frogs may not hibernate at all and can be heard peeping during the winter months. The shallow pools and ponds from which they call almost always have reeds, bushes, or weeds growing out of the water.

The females join the males in April. While many frogs lay their eggs in masses, the female peeper lays one at a time. She attaches each one to the stem of a plant under the water or even on the bottom of the pond. She may lay anywhere from several hundred to a thousand eggs.

By the end of May, all the females have laid their eggs, and most of the adult spring peepers leave the water. Now you will have trouble finding these small amphibians because they have stopped calling. They reach lengths of only three-quarters of an inch to one and a quarter inches. Also, they hide in or under bushes and leaves, which makes them even harder to find.

Most spring peepers are light brown to olive-grey. On the back two dark-brown stripes cross to form an X.

Spring peepers eat small insects, worms, and snails. Much of their hunting takes place on the ground, although these amphibians can climb well. The disks on their toes help peepers to crawl up bushes, long reeds, and trees.

While the adults hunt and hide in the woods, the eggs and tadpoles develop rapidly. The eggs swell as the larvae grow and the tadpoles emerge in one or two weeks. A tadpole may be an inch in length, which is a good size for the larva of such a small frog. In about three months metamorphosis is complete. The young peepers then leave the water to live on land just as the adults do.

Spring peepers are most active at night. A male can jump a foot and a half. This is a remarkable leap for such a small animal. Cool fall evenings slow the peeper down. In October in areas where it hibernates, it crawls under ground litter of leaves and bark, or under a log or stone.

In the United States, spring peepers are found throughout the states east of the Mississippi, though only in the northern part of Florida. They range as far west as eastern Texas and Oklahoma in the south and central Iowa and Minnesota in the north. Canada has peepers in south-eastern Manitoba, across southern and much of northern Ontario, in Quebec, and throughout the Maritime Provinces except for Newfoundland.

Gray Treefrog

Gray treefrogs like to live high above the ground. They climb among the branches of small trees and bushes and there they watch and wait, ready to lash out with their tongues to catch insects.

From its name, you might expect the gray treefrog to be grey, but this isn't necessarily true. It is one of the remarkable animals that can change colour. On a tree trunk or limb, the gray treefrog will be greyish brown to grey. On a leaf it becomes green. The back has dark blotches, the largest of which might remind you of a star. The undersides of the hind legs are bright orange. Under each eye this amphibian has a light spot.

The gray treefrog looks especially toadlike. It has a thickish body and a bumpy skin. Most toads, however, would seem like giants beside it. It is only one and a quarter to two and a quarter inches long.

In Canada, a few colonies of gray treefrogs live in southern New Brunswick, but naturalists fear these are vanishing. The main range includes south-western Quebec and southern Ontario, while some gray tree-frogs live in south-eastern Manitoba.

In the United States, they are found east of the Mississippi River except for northern Maine and southern Florida. West of the Mississippi they extend to the eastern edge of North Dakota in the north and to eastern Texas in the south.

Like many amphibians, gray treefrogs must go to water at egg-laying time. After they come out of hibernation in April, the males gather around shallow pools in the evening and make trilling calls. Each trilled note may last up to three seconds.

A female lays a thousand to two thousand eggs. She scatters them here and there in clusters of thirty to fifty. After four or five days they hatch. The tadpoles turn into frogs in six to eight weeks. The webs between their toes are small, but, as they are climbers, they have well-developed disks on their toes.

Many gray treefrogs come down from the trees and bushes early in the fall. By late September or early October they all have found hollows in rotting stumps or between the roots of trees in which to sleep through the cold weather. Some hibernate in hollows in the forks of trees.

American Toad

"Trr-r-r-r-r, trr-r-r-r." What a lovely trilling! You might expect it to come from one of the attractive frogs. But instead it comes from the homely "hoptoad". The balloon-like vocal sac under its lower jaw trembles and vibrates to the rhythm of its trilling. Its mouth remains tightly shut, which is true of all toads and frogs when they call.

The gardener should be particularly happy to hear this toad around the shallow pools near his land. The more toads in the garden, the fewer insects there will be to eat the vegetables. Every night an American toad catches dozens of insects with its sticky, two-inch tongue. Also it may eat an occasional slug or spider.

The American toad is the most common toad of eastern North America. All of the New England and the other north-eastern states have this amphibian, as do the Midwestern states east of the Mississippi River. It will be seen as far south as northern Mississippi, Alabama, and Georgia. It also lives in Minnesota, Iowa, Missouri, and eastern Kansas.

Canada has the American toad in south-eastern Manitoba, throughout central Ontario, and into northern Quebec, Labrador, and the Maritime Provinces. Look for it around shallow waters, even in ditches, in April and May when it is calling. After that, you will find it in gardens, woods, fields, city lots, and up to a mile high on mountain slopes. It stays out of the sun under leaves, boards, or bushes, but when evening stretches across the land it starts to hunt.

It travels by taking little hops. Its thick body and shortish legs aren't suitable for froglike leaps. It may hop less than a hundred feet in one night.

The American toad has a dry, lumpy skin. Some people fear they will get warts from handling a toad, but this is impossible.

Behind each eye, the American toad has a small bump. This is a gland from which the amphibian can secrete a whitish liquid. If this liquid gets in the mouth or eyes of another animal, it causes a burning sensation.

This toad reaches a length of between two and four inches. The larger ones are females and are the most colourful. Males are usually a muddy grey to brown, with dark blotches and dark warts. Females may be reddish brown to brownish green, with dark blotches and warts that range from brown to yellow.

Each female lays her eggs one after another in two long strings. A string may become sixty or seventy feet long before the female rests. By the time she is through laying, a female will have produced four to ten thousand eggs.

Black tadpoles hatch in three days to two weeks, and they promptly swim to the shallowest parts of their pools. Those that are not eaten by birds, insects, frogs, fish, turtles, and snakes develop into toads about half an inch long in two and a half weeks to two months. As soon as they become toads, the young go onto the land.

In October, American toads dig down into loose soil. Once they are under the frost level, they go to sleep for the winter.

Plains Spadefoot

If you don't mind getting wet, look for spadefoot toads during a heavy spring or summer rain. During dry spells, you wouldn't know these amphibians are in your neighbourhood. But when rain drenches the land, they come out of hiding.

On the prairies east of the Rocky Mountains, you will hear the plains spadefoot calling between February and August, but in Canada it will not start calling until May. Listen for a coarse, bleatlike grunt or a short, snore-like trill in southern Alberta and southwestern Saskatchewan. During or just after a hard rain you can also hear this call in Montana, North and South Dakota, Wyoming, Colorado, Nebraska, Kansas, Oklahoma, New Mexico, and northern and western Texas.

As the males call, the females hop toward the unmusical sounds. The eggs may be laid in large puddles or shallow ditches as well as in small ponds. Since puddles and ditches dry up between rains, the female must lay all her eggs in one to two days.

Each female produces a few hundred eggs. She lays them in bunches held together by jelly and attaches them to stalks of weeds. One clump may contain ten to a hundred eggs. The eggs hatch in two or three days, at which time a brownish, greenish, or somewhat golden tadpole appears.

The legs of the tadpole grow while the tail remains quite noticeable. Even if the pool dries up before metamorphosis ends, the spadefoot can survive if its lungs have developed. It crawls about on its short legs, pulling its tail behind it. Other toads and frogs sometimes go on land before their tails completely disappear, but they don't do this as often as the plains spadefoot does.

Once out of water, the plains spadefoot avoids moist places until it is ready to lay or fertilize eggs. On land it hunts insects by night. As dawn approaches, it digs into loose or sandy soil. Morning after morning a spadefoot toad returns to a burrow it has used before. Its life centres around this one spot.

A grown plains spadefoot will be an inch and a half to two inches long. Its skin lacks the wartiness of a true toad, yet is less smooth than the skin of a frog. Its colour is greyish to muddy brown, with a slight greenish colour. Small dark-brown to nearly black spots are scattered thickly over its back.

If you can look at a plains spadefoot's eye, you will see a pupil that seems to be standing on end. This vertical (up-and-down) pupil tells you the amphibian isn't a true toad. True toads have horizontal (side-to-side) pupils. Between its eyes, the plains spadefoot has a bump which is called a boss.

The feet of the plains spadefoot are thick compared with the feet of true toads and frogs. The webs grow nearly to the end of the short toes.

Just behind the shortest toes on the bottom of each hind foot grows a tough, wedge-shaped bump or "spade". Its sharp edge helps the plains spadefoot as the toad digs backwards into the ground. The dirt is not thrown out of the burrow as the spadefoot digs. The soft sandy soil falls in over the toad's body and covers the animal. In this way, the toad escapes the heat of the day.

Some time in September or October the plains spadefoot digs until it is three or four feet below the surface. There it goes to sleep and won't come out again until February or later.

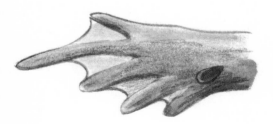

Blue-spotted Salamander

Salamanders are small, shy, secretive creatures, and for most people they are much harder to find than frogs or toads. Unlike frogs and toads, they are voiceless, only giving a small squeak when picked up.

The blue-spotted salamander is a mole salamander. As the second name suggests, it spends most of its life under the ground. It lives in wooded areas around swamps and along slow-flowing streams, or near shallow ponds. The ground in such places remains moist and provides the worms and soft-bodied insects the salamander needs. On rainy nights in late spring or summer, blue-spotted salamanders may dig up from their burrows to hunt on top of the ground.

In eastern North America, no other mole salamander lives so far north. These hardy salamanders can be found in Quebec and Ontario up to James Bay, and in a small area in southern Labrador. They live throughout the Atlantic provinces except for the

103

island of Newfoundland. Toward the west, they reach into south-eastern Manitoba.

Large numbers of blue-spotted salamanders live in the United States around the Great Lakes. From eastern Minnesota they range east and south across the midwest to West Virginia and northern Virginia, and northward through Pennsylvania, New York, and throughout New England.

The adults are bluish-black spotted with white and blue flecks. They have lighter bellies. In some, usually the largest, the blue spots can hardly be seen. They grow to a length of four or six inches. These amphibians can live twelve to eighteen years.

Warm rains of March and April bring these mole salamanders from their tunnels. Small groups of them collect in shallow water where a male courts a female. The female lays a few to thirty eggs at one time. She usually attaches them to a weed or stick. Perhaps she will lay up to four hundred eggs in one night. Some females stay with their eggs, but the blue-spotted salamander will leave after they are laid.

In two weeks to a month, the eggs hatch, revealing larvae an inch to two inches long. They grow to a length of about three inches in three to five months while developing legs and lungs. Now their blue spots are particularly noticeable. Once they turn into sala-

manders, they leave the water and dig into the soft
ground.

Salamanders are tailed amphibians. At first glance
you might confuse them with lizards, but unlike the
reptiles, salamanders have a smooth skin and no claws.
Salamanders never have more than four toes on the
front feet; lizards usually have five.

Mudpuppy

Early settlers had the mistaken idea that these strange silent salamanders barked. They named them water-dogs or, more commonly, mudpuppies.

These salamanders never change from the larval form, even though they grow to a length of eight to fifteen inches. They never lose their gills. All its life, a mudpuppy must remain in the water.

Usually the mudpuppy stays well below the surface of the water. There it catches crayfish, water insects, fish, and snails, or eats water plants and the eggs of other creatures. To swim, it waves its tail back and forth. It has four short legs which are useful in crawling on the bottom of ponds, lakes, streams, and rivers. It has four toes on each foot.

The feet and legs are grey to reddish-brown, as are the sides and back, while the belly is pale grey. On the sides toward the tail and on the tail itself appear blue-black spots, and the belly, too, may have dark flecks scattered here and there. The gills are reddish.

Three pairs of gill arches grow out of each side of the neck. They are heavily "feathered" and the mudpuppy waves the plumes to move the water over the gills and get the oxygen it needs to breathe.

By day the mudpuppy usually sleeps under rocks in its watery home or burrows into the mud. At night it hunts for food. However, if the water is muddy and thick with weeds this amphibian will prowl about at any hour.

A mudpuppy doesn't have ordinary ears that stand up on the outside of its head. Instead it has internal ear bones that are sensitive to vibrations. The lower jaw of this salamander picks up vibrations and transmits them to the ear bones. For this reason, the mudpuppy sleeps with its chin resting on the rock or mud where it is napping.

In October or November, mudpuppies mate. Then they burrow under rocks or into the mud to sleep through the winter. In April they become active again and the females go to the clearest part of the water or to a place where there is a good current. Clear and swiftly flowing waters provide more oxygen than muddy, still pools.

In May or June a female mudpuppy lays a hundred to two hundred eggs. One at a time she attaches them to the underside of a rock, where they hang like tear drops in a coating of jelly. She remains close at hand to drive away enemies. The eggs hatch in a month and a half to two months.

The newly hatched larvae are about three-quarters of an inch long. During their first few years they may be yellow and have black stripes down their backs and sides, but these disappear by the time they are five to seven years old.

If you live in northern Mississippi or in Tennessee, Missouri, Kentucky, West Virginia, Ohio, Indiana, Illinois, Iowa, Minnesota, Wisconsin, Michigan, Pennsylvania, New York, or western New England, you are in mudpuppy country. These amphibians also can be found in eastern Kansas and the Dakotas. In Canada they range from south-eastern Manitoba through southern Ontario and Quebec.

Red-spotted Newt

Some salamanders go through a larval stage and then develop into amphibians that live on land, such as the blue-spotted salamander. Others never grow out of the larval stage and always remain in the water, such as the mudpuppy. Most strange, perhaps, are the salamanders that pass through three stages. One of these is the red-spotted newt.

Between February and May, adult red-spotted newts gather in weedy sections of shallow bodies of water. The male discharges a jellylike substance into the water. The female takes the jelly to where she will lay her eggs, for it will fertilize them. One at a time, she lays two hundred to four hundred eggs and fastens them to the stems and leaves of weeds. She lets the eggs go unguarded.

In three weeks to a month, the eggs hatch and tiny larvae a quarter of an inch long appear. They look somewhat like tadpoles but in two days their front legs begin to grow. Their hind legs appear a day or two

111

later, whereas the tadpoles of frogs and toads develop their hind legs first. During the next three months, red-spotted newts reach a length of one to three inches and lose their gills. Now they must go on land to live.

You have a better chance of seeing red-spotted newts than other salamanders because of this land-living stage. Watch for them in the Maritime Provinces (except for Newfoundland) and in southern Quebec and Ontario. They live throughout New England and in the states along the Atlantic coast down to central North Carolina.

Away from the coast, watch for them in northern South Carolina, Georgia, and Alabama. They don't range as far west as the Mississippi River, but you can find them in much of Tennessee, Kentucky, and Indiana, and all of Michigan, Ohio, and West Virginia.

When they crawl from the water, these amphibians are a bright orange-red. Red spots ringed with black can easily be seen on their backs and sides. At this stage they are called red efts. They will remain in wooded areas for two to four years while they mature.

Red efts protect themselves by secreting a poison from their skins that burns the mouths of other animals. When winter comes, they hibernate under rocks, logs, or masses of leaves.

When fully mature, the red efts return to the water.

They are now three to four inches long and will grow very little more. They have also changed colour and have developed a broad swimming tail. Their backs are olive to dark green or brown while their bellies are yellowish dotted with black. Bright-red spots can still be seen along their bodies. Some red-spotted newts do not pass through the eft stage but change directly from larvae into aquatic adults.

In the water and on land, they catch insects. They also eat worms, snails, leeches, and the eggs and tadpoles of frogs and toads. Perhaps they serve man most by eating mosquito larvae.

You may be able to see fully grown red-spotted newts in winter. They are active in the water at lower temperatures than many amphibians. Some of them remain active all year, even though the surface of the water in which they live freezes solid. Where ice and water are clear, look down into a pond or lake. You may see a red-spotted newt walking along the bottom.

Tiger Salamander

A tiger salamander is an amphibian with a skin that is generally black but spotted or barred with yellow or creamy white. It lives east of the Rockies and all the way to the south Atlantic seaboard. Most of its life is spent in tunnels, for it is one of the mole salamanders. In the north look for it in southern Saskatchewan and British Columbia and in central and southern Alberta.

You will have to look for tiger salamanders in early spring when they make their overland journeys to their mating sites. These amphibians dig out of their burrows and migrate to the water. If you see them at this time, you will notice that they twist from side to side as they walk much as lizards do. Usually they cover ground more slowly than the reptiles.

The female lays twenty to seventy eggs in a jellylike clump and attaches them to weeds under water. This water may be alkaline — that is, it has the salts of various minerals dissolved in it. Such water would kill some amphibians, but the tiger salamander can stand it.

After two or three weeks, larvae less than an inch long swim free and begin to look for mosquito larvae and other small insects to eat. The salamander larvae usually change into their final stage in two and a half to three months. When lungs have replaced their gills, they must leave the water.

At this time tiger salamanders locate deserted burrows of other animals or dig tunnels of their own. Like many other amphibians, they move about at night. After dark they catch worms and insects.

Spotted tiger salamanders can be twelve inches long when fully grown. If they avoid snakes, skunks, raccoons, badgers, weasels, and large birds, they probably live twelve to fifteen years.

Some tiger salamanders don't complete metamorphosis. They keep their gills and live in water all their lives. No one knows for sure why this happens. Some naturalists think the water in which they live contains a low amount of oxygen compared to other elements. Other men who study animal life think it is because certain elements, such as iodine, are missing from the water. When these larvae are moved to other waters, they frequently finish changing into land-living adults.

Learn to know all amphibians and reptiles in your vicinity. You will find them to be fascinating, colourful animals.